Fumigated

Also by Ioana Petrescu and published by Ginninderra Press
Persuading Plato

Ioana Petrescu

Fumigated

> Would you try it for, say, six months, a poem every week?
> Preferably set in the form of prose, so as not to offend anyone.
> – Anthony Burgess

To my parents

Acknowledgements

Magazines
*The Adelaide Review, Southerly, Redoubt, SideWaLk, The Bunyip,
The New England Review*

Anthologies
*Friendly Street 24, Friendly Street 25, The Colonial Athens,
Sleeping Under a Grand Piano*

Street art exhibition
VIEW 2000

Radio
Radio 5UV, Radio 5AN, ABC Radio National (Poetica).

Cover photograph by Emil Petrescu shows Catherine's Gate, Braşov (part of the medieval town fortress).

Fumigated
ISBN 978 1 74027 082 3
Copyright © Ioana Petrescu 2001

First published 2001
Reprinted 2016

Ginninderra Press
PO Box 3461 Port Adelaide 5015
www.ginninderrapress.com.au

Contents

Introduction	7
From East to West	9
Romania, Christmas 1989	11
Europe by night	14
Almost like a virgin	17
Weeks before revolution	19
East meets West	20
Post-enlightenment tourism	21
Saying goodbye	23
Fumigated	24
My privacy	25
Fax from home	26
Definition	27
We breathed in	28
Preparing the family dinner	29
The plumber's impressions of Europe	30
Streets	31
Fragrances	32
In a row	33
Modelling	34
At night	35
Some facts about Little Red Riding Hood…	36
Song for my son	37
Shaped by three tongues	38
Underpinnings	39
Deep structure	41
The visit	42
Chatelaine	44
Owl	45

Creek	46
Metaphysics	47
***	48
Sidewalk café	49
Brief treatise on academics and their ways	50
Underpinnings	51
Creative process	52
Writer's block	53
Wounded by language	54
Poetry workshop	55
Transaction	56
Arid	57
Plato and Aristotle at the market	58
Folkrock letter	59
Love and things	**61**
Mystery woman	63
SBS afterplay	64
Alma Mater	66
Fairy tale	67
On *Cleo* quoting *Allure*	68
Words	69
In a dream	70
PMS	71
On request	72
Munch's man	73
Poem	74
Rhetoric	75
Sacred	76
Teenagers at the movies	77
Free	78
Song	79

Introduction

As a migrant from Romania, Ioana Petrescu brings a lyrical but wry examination of her new landscape and its people.

The very title of the collection, *Fumigated*, tellingly describes one of the odd experiences many new arrivals to Australia have encountered as their introduction to this country: the ritual drenching of the cabin with aerosol. Her responses to the new environment are located, not in grand generalisations or 'big' definitions, but in an amused and sometimes delighted study of tiny matters of detail –the way of light, the chatter of a plumber, suburban nuances. Her lyric talent is contained in the very brevity and wit of her cadences, as well as in the more extended poems which take a theme and explore it with deft precision.

The book begins with a group of powerful, disturbing poems about her homeland. These form the undeniable base upon which the poems of discovery and immediate response spring out with their sense of play and their secret silences.

These are not poems of exile and suffering. They are poems of discovery.

Tom Shapcott

From East to West

> The only reason why people want to be
> masters of the future is to change the past.
> – Milan Kundera

Romania, Christmas 1989

You've known this street for thirty years,
its people, its colours, smells and sounds.
Tonight you hear a new sound –
a machine gun,
in your street,
as if they're shooting a movie.
Your mind, still working, tells you
infra-red machine guns
detect body heat in the dark,
so you put the baby
down on the carpet
and cover him with
your body,
gently, not to crush him,
so he can breathe,
and hope that the guns
will be fooled into detecting just one heartbeat,
and if bullets should come
they'll stop in your body
and spare your baby.

The machine guns break
from time to time
and the silence is even
more frightening.
Babies' cries can be heard
a long way in this silence,
and those people shoot in the direction of noises,
but your baby is now asleep.

You know the feeding schedule.
Every six hours offer both breasts, alternately,
no intermediary feedings between regular times
or at night, so as not to spoil his appetite –
both modern paediatricians
and old midwives
agree on this,
but you still offer your breast
when he wakes up,
so he doesn't cry
in the silence.
But your milk's just gone sour
and the baby turns his nose
in disgust – horrible taste.
Then your milk stops flowing altogether.

On the morning news
you see a morgue;
in other streets other mothers
who have instinctively shielded
their children with their bodies
have been less lucky;
modern technology bullets
through one body and kills two
at a time.

They only shoot after dark.

Next night, not knowing any better,
you hide in the darkest corner of your home
and you cover your baby again
with your body
and offer your milkless breast
as a pacifier
and try not to think
about anything.

They're shooting again in your street
and machine guns sound surreal here
among medieval walls.

Next morning you don't watch the news.
The milk van and the bread van
arrive at the corner deli
and neighbours you've always known
go out in the street.
They don't talk to each other.
Then there's night and day again
in your street
and you count days
by the nights.

Europe by night

The letter is from the West.
Dear colleague, it says,
we have the great pleasure
of inviting you to our conference.

The plane a remote financial dream
for an Eastern European lecturer,
I buy a ticket second-class
for a night train.

The smugglers, prostitutes
and black-market labourers
filter their looks through eyelashes
watching me, the incongruous passenger,
but decide I must be harmless
once they see my books and pens.

They have stories to tell
about families, little brothers and sisters
in need of clothing and feeding.
My patient listening skills are rewarded
with full-time protection –
no harm is to be done
to the teacher travelling alone
by night train.

They relax.
The smugglers compare prices
and information on what's hot
on the market.
The prostitute offers whisky
to everyone in the train compartment,
and the black-market labourer
shows me a photo of his wife
and three kids.
Last time his job was
to climb a ladder, drill holes
and fix parts to a prefab wall
at forty degrees Celsius;
the money bought pigs and chicken
for the family farm –
his wife and kids look after them.

I arrive.
They wish me well
and the train disappears in the dark.

At the conference people read papers
and then have a festive dinner.
We eat caviar
and salmon accompanied by chilled white wine.
The lecturer from the North misses her Rottweilers.
The lecturer from the South is young and petite,
dressed in white lace, and very busy
massaging the ego of a Head of Department.
He's brought over his pretty second wife
and is looking around for his next.
A doctor in philosophy has just paved
the road from the highway to the house
he bought at the foot of a hill,
far from the city's 'frets and fumes'.
I keep quiet. My dress
is from two fashions before and I hope
people will either not notice
or think I'm eccentric.

Shortly before midnight
I have to leave to catch the last train.
Take a taxi, they say,
it's not safe out there
at this hour.

Almost like a virgin

I can hear them in the dark.

Is she dead? asks a young nurse.
No, there's a pulse, but hush,
they can hear every word in this state.
Let's call a second doctor. Let's do a caesarean.
No, she won't make it.
But she can't push any more,
says the young voice.
A new voice replies:
I'll do it for her.

*I'm cold, I've been saying this for a while,
but they can't hear me from here
in the dark.
Maybe I should move my lips,
I could try to do this for them…
here, then there…
crossing boundaries
again and again…
I need the energy.*

The doctor climbs on the table next to me
and pushes his elbow right through my chest
like a stake through a vampire.
My body splits into two:
the heart bursts through my throat
and beats again – this time on my tongue;
the baby shoots out into the world
splitting my body
into quarters of halves.

I'm cold, I manage to tell them,
careful not to spit out my heart.
Someone throws a blanket over me
and crosses herself.
The young nurse
vomits her womanly instincts in a sink –
I bet she'll think twice before
each future fuck.

I can see him now. He's wiping the cold sweat
from my forehead.
Welcome back, gorgeous, he jokes,
in a couple of months
you'll be like a virgin.

Weeks before revolution

Friday is just another day.
Saturday is another workday.
Sunday is a day before
another week.
Monday is philharmonic concert day.
Tuesday is another day
like Wednesday, but Thursday
is black-market day –
coffee for my mother,
meat, eggs and maybe chocolate for the family,
contraceptives if we've run out of those
(days are long, nights even longer),
and also nice things for doctors, just in case –
soap for a cough, cigarettes for a cold,
whisky or crystal ware for
more severe things – touch wood.

East meets West

The visitor was treated as a VIP:
he was from the West.
After the festive lunch
and the toasts
vowing everlasting friendship,
he was given a guide
with vast knowledge about the place.

The guide took him to visit
the old town,
the city gates
the medieval water ditch
and the cathedral,
where a world famous artist
was playing the organ.

The visitor thanked them nicely
and said
'Now that we've got
the boring part of the program
behind us,
let's go to the mall
and then to a pub, maybe.
There's still enough time
to have some fun
and save the rest of the day.'

Post-enlightenment tourism

After the fall of the Wall
those friends of mine decided to visit
the West.
He put on his best suit and tie,
and she decided to wear make-up
and her family jewels
saved by her grandmother
during the great nationalisation of goods.

Carrying a Zenith camera
built on steel chassis,
they admired the historical centre,
and wanted a photo of them both
in front of the cathedral.

He approached a lady
and putting on his best accent
he asked her whether
she would be so kind as to
press the button.
The lady gave him a terrified look
and ran away.

He approached a man next,
and asked politely for the same favour.
The man said something about calling the police
and ran away.

Later they wanted
to know the time.

She decided that his accent
was not good enough,
so she took the assignment upon herself.
'Could you tell me the time, please?'
'Excuse me, what time is it?'
'What's the time?'
People just gave her odd looks
and walked away.

Finally, a nice old lady
told her the time.
It was fairly late
both in the East and the West.

Saying goodbye

I made little holes in the earth
and put marigold seeds in each.
I'm leaving, Daddy, I told the seeds
while I was covering them with earth.
These are marigolds, they are strong,
they'll keep in the sun
and rain will feed them.
I'm leaving and won't come back
from the other hemisphere.
I'm leaving but my marigolds
will look after your grave.

Fumigated

The new place assesses me
with circumspection.
Perhaps fumigation might
conjure the stranger in me.
So here they come, spray cans in hand.
Now we are – more or less –
ready for one another.

My privacy

I share my private existence
with nineteen neighbours
a gum tree
and a kookaburra.

At five a.m. a bird rings –
or is it the phone? –
they must be ringing
from back home.

It's the bird.

In the other hemisphere
my family prepares to go to sleep.

Fax from home

Transaction? Of identity perhaps.
Transmission? Only words.
Number? Of sleepless nights and jet-lagged days.
Date? March. Autumn. Or spring.
Destination?
Duration?
Mode? Normal, it says.
    It's normal, I tell myself.
Result? Urinate in this plastic cup, please.
    OK.
    I can stay. According to the plastic cup
    I'm a safe, healthy migrant.

Definition

Otherness is when
in spite of speaking the language
you need footnotes
for your thoughts, words and gestures
and whatever else
you might wish to convey.

We breathed in

the vapours from spray cans.
I've never met again the people
who flew with me on that trip
for forty-eight hours, but,
I suspect,
there must be a plane load
of fumigated poets around.

This summer and winter
three years and a half from that day,
while fir trees grown by my memory
were being covered in snow again,
purple jacarandas
spoke to me for the first time
the familiar language of beauty.

Preparing the family dinner

For Emil

My thoughts were cluttering the kitchen sink
>*sink at the brink of thought*
>*multiplied by birds*
>*flying into the colour*
>*of dishwashing liquid.*

I chopped a few fresh similes
>*my love is like your love*
>*mirror and prism*
>*of tangent illusions – our love*
>*like no one else's love.*

'Just add water' it said on the package
>*I added clear water. On looking down*
>*I could see the day I was born*
>*people fretting around me*
>*cutting my umbilical cord.*

We washed our hands before dinner
>*once for luck*
>*twice for luck*
>*and once for the pebbles*
>*rounded by the sea.*

The plumber's impressions of Europe

So, what's wrong with that tap?
I ask.
Nothing ma'am, just bloody bludgers
didn't fix it properly,
and, by the way,
what's that accent of yours?
I tell him.
I've been there, he says.
So how was it? I ask.
I wouldn't know ma'am,
just flew in, was meant to stay a week,
felt sick on the plane, they took me straight
to a hospital there, can't remember a thing,
next day they put me on a plane,
sent me back to Vienna.
So how was Vienna?
Don't know, he says – he was sick.
But I've been to London, big town, nice pubs,
met another Aussie, from Melbourne of all places,
but he was quite all right, I suppose,
good bloke, liked a pub crawl.
I've also seen Prague, beautiful town,
then worked a bit on a farm in Israel,
got me some money and flew to the States.
Your tap should be right now, he says,
gathers his tools, calls his dog,
and goes to his next job.

Streets

The gum tree guards the suburban silence.

I close my eyes. *Cars and trucks,*
tokens of my street
dust and burnt gas
the smells of my childhood.

I play hopscotch in the street, the drawing
marks my portion of sidewalk
passers-by go in wide circles,
respect my territory.

The grass on my front lawn has been mown recently
all grass blades are orderly, tidy,
presenting their suburban-green salute
to no one.

A kookaburra laughs at my mind-set –
city girl, city girl, play hopscotch if you can
in the squares of blue sky
drawn by the gum tree.

Fragrances

Quince – perfume of autumn,
my mother's favourite jam
boiling on the stove,
filling the kitchen with warmth
on a late afternoon.

Snow – chilling my nostrils,
filling the streets,
the promise of ice-skating plus
tangerines imported by Santa.

Lavender – first lover,
his mother, pedantic nurse,
kept entire fields dried
in wardrobes and drawers.

Books – fragrance of addiction;
roses – fragrance of marriage;
milk – fragrance of the new-born baby;
freesias for my birthday –
fragrances of the old home.

In a row

I remember my father's shoes,
always shining but worn down.
All spare money was spent on me –
my schools, my language tutors, my shoes.
People shook their heads disapprovingly.
Leave her a house or a bank account, they said,
who cares how many languages one speaks, if poor.

My father died young of a heart attack.

I polished his shoes as he'd liked them to be
and then lined them up in a row. Two days before
my father had taken one of his boots to a cobbler –
I never knew who.
Beneath a heavy winter coat bearing his shape
my father's left boot
unheedingly finished the row.

Modelling

The statue of Johannes Honterus, great Transylvanian humanist and correspondent of Erasmus von Rotterdam, stood in front of the school. In one hand he held a book, the other hand motioned with the forefinger. To me he looked like a nice grandpa, so I used to sit on his sun-heated pedestal, a book in one hand, a ham sandwich in the other.

At night

Footsteps. A hushed voice on the corridor.
My little son bravely dispels
shadows of night-time demons
while going to the toilet.

Some facts about Little Red Riding Hood you always wanted to know but were afraid to ask

For Sergiu

After the Wolf swallowed Grandma and Little Red Riding Hood they spent some time in his bowels. Why doesn't it say whether they had a nice shower when they came out?

And then, the wolf episode must have been tough on her. I mean, you know, being swallowed by a wolf and then rescued sounds like a hell of an experience.

And what about that hunter haunting Grandma's lovely place in the woods? He'd heard some loud snoring, he said. Now come on, who would barge into a neighbour's house with the poor excuse of having heard some loud snoring?

Oh yeah, and then there's the basket thing – cookies and wine, remember? That Grandma was supposed to knock off a whole bottle of wine by herself in her lonely hut, in the middle of nowhere.

Gee, isn't that a terrible story, this Little Red Riding Hood?

Song for my son

My swollen belly moved –
a bony heel brushed against my heart
and stopped in my ribs.
I sang him a song – swim my baby, swim,
soon you'll be pushing and brushing the air.

My baby cried – it was cold outside.
I sang him a song – I know it's cold, my boy.
Soon you'll grow up, you will be a man
and will seek the warmth
of another woman.

My son leaned on me and I nearly fell.
I sang him a song – be strong my boy,
my only strength is my song for you,
its words lie on shelves
of water and air.

Shaped by three tongues

Blown by the wind,
before it sways its way to the ground
I've already named it –
frunză/leaf/Blatt.

I pick it up, fold it in three,
        îi modific dimensiunile și forma
        I change its dimensions and form
        ich ändere seine Maßen und Form.

Now a stranger in its own skin,
I have to admit it still looks
like the old leaf.

Underpinnings

> Colourless green ideas sleep furiously.
> – Noam Chomsky, *Syntactic Structures*

Deep structure

For Randall

The world lies on the shell
of a big brown turtle,
said the old woman.
And what does the turtle lie on?
asked the young man.
Well, of course, on the shell
of another big brown turtle.
And what would that turtle lie on?
he asked.
The old woman looked at him sheepishly.
Oh, young man, you can't fool me –
it's turtles
all the way down.

The visit

All art is useless.
– Oscar Wilde

I've decided to visit
a few of my older acquaintances, so I'm having tea
with Dorian Gray – I at the table,
he in his portrait. His fine features
mock me from both the wall and the teacup –
not even the tea can break into ripples
his perfect reflection. My own face is old, very old,
and it's also there in the teacup behind
Dorian Gray's image. Perhaps I'm pleased to see that,
in fact I've never been beautiful, so I sip at my tea
and ask him how he's been lately.
I can feel my hair growing, millimetre by millimetre,
and by the time my thoughts become audible
the butler brings in some biscuits.
My umbrella is dripping in a corner,
'Open it,' says Dorian Gray,
'it'll dry faster,' so I stand,
walk to the corner where the umbrella is
and open it. Bright yellow instantly lights up the attic.

'You know,' says Dorian Gray,
'years ago I had a crush on you, but somehow
you never seemed to notice the rich handsome lads,
only the smart ones.' I look down in my teacup.
What can I tell him? I liked his perfect features,
but I had read the book so I knew they'd become
wrinkled and covered in beard. I stand up,
thank him for the lovely evening,
shut my umbrella and leave. The butler
opens the door for me and tells me
'So nice to see you here Mrs P. Mr G
does not receive that many visits from
older acquaintances lately.' 'Indeed?' I reply,
but in fact I'm not listening. I'm looking intently
out there in the street, down to the pavement
where I can clearly see my face
in a puddle.

Chatelaine

I have a bunch of keys
in my purse.
One opens Khalif Haroun al Rashid's
room of wonders –
the one where he keeps
real size jade elephants
and pomegranates made of garnets.
Another is from my office
where I keep books and files.
The big key with a flower pattern
is from the house of thought –
men and women
sit there around the coffee table
and speak about Freud and Riemann.
And this little key here
was given to me for safekeeping
forever, I believe.
As the years go by
I add more and more keys;
touching them in my purse
makes me feel secure.
I can open more and more
doors.

Owl

Shriek of wisdom
parting the dark –
a flutter of wings.

Creek

If you were the creek
you'd feel hibernating snakes
on your body,
water would be your blood,
reeds would be your hair.

The cool wind of the night
would bring owls for you –
wise by day, indecent at this hour.
Staring at you with hypocritical eyes
they'd teach you the murky shallowness
of proverbs.

Metaphysics

The moon is the yolk
of an egg I'll never see.

In my backyard birds occupy spaces.
When they fly away no gaps are left –
fluid space flows back in itself
as if never cut through
by wings.

***

When I sleep,
the weight of the stars on my forehead
becomes unbearable,
so I try
to send them back in the sky
pushing them with a dream.

Sidewalk café

Don't sit at my table. I'm not
good company today. I've lost a cloud
and the count of the leaves
in that tree over there.

You see, when a woman passes by and looks
in the café window, I look too and see myself,
my failure to catch clouds and count
leaves of neighbourhood trees.

Men rarely stop to admire their reflection in the window.
Perhaps they have an inner eye, just one, like Cyclops,
so all they need to do is look inside, and it's fine.
See, I can't do this.

I need achievements – so many clouds were caught
between this and that hour in such and such streets.
It's a matter of being organised,
of working with things
and not against them.

As you can see, I've got
things to sort out myself,
so please
don't sit at my table.

Brief treatise on academics and their ways

How do academics think?
They throw pebbles in waters and they watch the circles growing out of one another. They choose a circle and try to pin it to the previous one, then to the next one, to the water, the water lilies and the dragonflies. By the time they finish, the water is still again, so they throw in more pebbles.

How do academics cry?
They write papers with long spindrifting sentences, speech serpentines frozen on A4 pages, font 12, Times New Roman.

How do academics feel?
From their hearts, arterial red cells rise up to the grey ones, they react together (it's just chemistry, really), then simply flow out of the body through the fingertips, sometimes as thought blueprints and at other times as blots on the page, depending on the size and shape of the pebbles thrown in the water.

Underpinnings

My teachers live on clouds
of clay –
their thoughts
trapped in brain circumvolutions,
pinned to their foreheads,
moulded
in clay.

I learn their language.

I try to pin my thoughts
to my skull –
my thoughts are butterflies.
I learn to mould
butterflies of clay.

They say,
when I graduate,
I'll receive from their hands
my own cloud of clay.

Creative process

Story #1:
Boy meets girl –
they fall in love,
they marry, have children
and live happily
ever after.
Publisher's reaction:
passé –
nobody will swallow this.

Story #2:
Partner meets partner –
they fall in love,
they do not marry
because they can't get a divorce.
Publisher's reaction:
too real –
nobody will want to know.

Story #3:
Green-eyed monster meets eerie girl
escaped from an underground lab
where an experiment went terribly wrong.
They fall in love
and figure out some kinky way
to have S E X.
Publisher's reaction:
bingo –
now we're in business.

Writer's block

I haven't written a poem since
last time I wrote a poem.

Fractions
of
poems
came
and
lasted
fractions
of
seconds

until I accidentally saw
an empty door frame
through an empty window
frame and thought

maybe I can still
write a poem

the poem which walks through no door
looks out through no window
and cuts right through this rarefied space
of unwritten poems.

Wounded by language

Don't look at me – I'm not a poet.
When I wake at night
words strive for freedom
and I liberate them on paper.

Don't look at me
when I wrestle with language.
It's embarrassing.
I've got bruises
from a synecdoche,
but oxymorons do much worse:
I was abused
when they realised
I was not a poet.

Don't be misled.
What you hear
are not lines and stanzas
they are just spells
I chant
while healing
after being wounded
by language.

Poetry workshop

'Truth, beauty and love
are ALL corny,'
says the lecturing poet.

He's got two silver rings on his left hand
and his silver bracelet gives a 'kling'
every time he gestures.
His white crinkled shirt is wide open
and a silver chain glistens
on his black chest hair.

'Truth is relative' – kling goes the bracelet,
'pure beauty doesn't exist' – kling again,
'and love…oh, please,
don't be sentimental.'

I press one hand on my corny heart
while I'm conscientiously
jotting down in my notebook
'the poet says don't write about love.'

Transaction

The bank employee gives me a knowing look –
uh-huh, so you wish to deposit some words?
Yes, I own a few, I admit fiddling with my pen.
You know, there's no interest for words, he says.
Actually there's a fee for
each coined word or newly minted phrase.
I like him. He's wearing a tie with koalas,
so I give him one of my words for free.
You'll get a monthly statement reflecting the state
of your words. Sign here, he says.
I write my name.
Already I'm owned by my own
words.

Arid

On reading Michael Meehan's *The Salt of Broken Tears*

In the middle of the city
is a desert.
He has learned
its corners and dunes,
knows he needs to put one foot
in front of the other
to stay alive.
Grit in his black leather shoes
(to match belt and briefcase)
rubs into blisters.
To escape desert stress
he says his name
loud and clear but
there's no one behind smiles
to confirm his identity.
Every morning at ten
he stops briefly –
black coffee still fools his thirst.
Call now, says the mirage
of a desert woman,
*buy and save –
build your house
on shifting sands,
purchase a four-wheel drive
exclusively designed
for desert treks.*
Hot sand slaps his mouth
and sticks to his grin.
Not a home did he erect
inside his nomadic body –
he buried there
his own pyramid.

Plato and Aristotle at the market

Some people prefer Platonic markets:
first you've got to find the place,
design the market and think –
tomatoes here, carrots there,
fruit over there, and along that wall
shiny windows for meat.
Then you'd bring in
tomatoes, carrots, fruit and meat
and place them neatly
in the previously designated areas.
This is your market place –
logical, orderly, clean –
you can come and make a fuss,
a bit of disorder,
it will just enhance
the quality of the project.

Others prefer Aristotelian markets:
come on, everyone, bring what you've got –
tomatoes, carrots, paw paws, rambutans,
you can stay anywhere you like,
dazzle your customers.
People get into a frenzy of buying.
Some of this – a bit of that –
more and more… Well,
markets will be markets.

Folkrock letter

Dear Eve, this morning at six a.m. sharp
I thought technology was fucked, for the electronic game
which is also my alarm-clock started beeping
and the shower was wet-wet-wet
but I still caught the bus with its usual students, elderly
people
and miniskirted employees with cellulite all over their thighs.
I dropped off my son at the kiss-and-drop area,
and again caught the bus,
for life, yeah, is but a journey
on a bloody bus. I'll ask for copyright clearance to say
that carless in Adelaide is after all
better than eyeless in Ghaza.

So I arrived at uni where I saw:
cockatoos on a rooftop,
ducks, a goose and a pelican
on the lake beneath the trees
fluttering and dancing in the breeze
(sorry Will).
As I reached my room
Eudora could use some help,
the computer died on me
and I decided to write to you at six p.m. sharp
because technology was fucked
and that made my day.

Love and things

> There isn't any formula or method.
> You learn to love by loving – by paying attention
> and doing what one thereby discovers has to be done.
> – Aldous Huxley

Mystery woman

Lying in bed at night
the woman thinks of all the wonderful things
she could have told him
but didn't.
Right at that moment
her nose starts itching.
And since she can't pick her nose,
roll a ball, flick it on the lampshade
precisely
AND talk –
she prefers to remain silent,
providing the man
with yet another enigma
of the mystery woman.

SBS afterplay

Curtains.
Some noises in the background.
We can't see anything
but the noises induce subliminal images –
THE last spasms.

Now we can see them.
They lie side by side
watching the ceiling.

Honey, says he, I've sweated
in my ears. No really,
I mean it, come on,
feel my left ear.

As she doesn't seem attracted
by this activity,
he takes her right forefinger
and determinedly introduces it into
his left ear.
Yeah, she says, it's sweaty all right,
and tries to pull out her finger
but, like I said, he's rather determined.

You should see my right ear, he says,
it's heaps sweatier, really.
By now, knowing that she's not going
to get away, she feels his right ear
and is shocked –
boy, that IS sweaty!

She voices her appreciation
and then resumes watching the ceiling.
Darling, she says, we really need to
repair that ceiling. No really,
I mean it, come on, have a look at
those cracks in the ceiling.

As he doesn't seem attracted
by this activity,
she takes his head in her hands and turns it
until he can properly see the cracks
in the ceiling.
Knowing that he's not going to get away,
he takes a long hard look at the ceiling
and is shocked –
boy, those ARE cracks!

Then he says, then she says,
then he says, then she says, then
the camera rolls to the curtains.

The End.

Alma Mater

One of the brightest students by far,
he rarely came to lectures
as he preferred erudite discussions at staff/student seminars
and specialist symposiums.
His appearance was always theatrical –
long coat, big hat,
large gestures and smiles.
He always managed to pass his exams
as he just knew so much, thought so much, said so much.
Linguists thought he'd become a language specialist,
literati thought he'd become a critic,
while philosophers pinned all their hopes on him dreaming to shine
at least in a footnote by their student.

No one noticed his absence for a while,
when, after months, a postcard arrived:
enormous white luxury line cruiser
in the middle of the baby-blue ocean.
Greetings, it said on the back,
thanks for sharing with me
all those helpful tricks of your knowledge.
I use language, literature, philosophy
and much, much psychology
on an everyday basis.
My relations with clients are excellent,
and my updated references refer
to my distinguished professionalism as
cultured, well-mannered and highly refined
line cruiser escort.

Fairy tale

Once upon a time
while she was washing clothes
on the banks of a river
the prince came
and fell in love with her.

Once upon a time
while she was cleaning the oven
the prince came and brought her
the lost glass slipper.

Once upon a time
while she was spinning gold in a humble hut
the prince came
and made her his princess.

Now, she lives in his castle.
Her room is full with the gold she spins,
with her ball gowns and her glass slippers.

The prince is out
hunting.

On *Cleo* quoting *Allure*

'12 per cent of Americans believe
that Joan of Arc
was Noah's wife.'

Twelve per cent of myself
would like to believe the same.
As far as I know
Noah was a nice man
of about five hundred years of age
who wouldn't have dreamed
of doing her any harm.
I have always admired
his ecological views.
But then again
I can't help thinking
that the bald eagle,
which he saved in his ark,
is endangered anyhow.
Would this mean that Joan of Arc
would have been endangered as well
whether she were Noah's wife
or not?

Words

As words enlace me
I imagine they'd stayed unspoken –
then, your tongue could break them down
into syllables, morphemes and phonemes
tracing them on my body
until I am able to feel
their meaning.

In a dream

Her dream was most bizarre.
She dreamt she was a huge female spider
brown and velvety.
All his eight legs were entwined with hers
and she felt his soft belly on her back
while he was loving her.

Then she dreamt she was a cloud
and he was a cloud.
When they met the lightning struck
down in the hills and the earth trembled
and trees burnt down
while he was loving her.

In her dream
she had her eyes wide open
looking deep into his eyes
while he was
loving her.

PMS

Spasms
like misfit orgasms –
a mind
waiting for
humiliation
to consume
itself
and fade
away.

On request

Shall I hum a song for you?
I could climb on the roof top
and hum my song from there.
You see, I'm a coward,
I wouldn't want everyone to know
I'm humming a song for you, and I guess
no one would see me up there.

Shall I write a letter for you?
I could use the wings of a bee,
the leaves of sage, and whiskers
of that cat roaming about in our neighbourhood.
Put on paper, I'm sure they'd make
all the difference.

Shall I turn around and go?
I could do it swiftly, you wouldn't even notice:
I'd just go humming with the cat
from rooftop to rooftop
bees' wings on my eyelids,
sage leaves in my hair.

Munch's man

What Munch didn't know
when he looked at his own painting
with his inward eye
was the fact that the portrayed man
turned his face from the beach
to look at a woman.
Munch's vision, truncated by gloom,
could not incorporate
her form in his space.

Poem

I just wanted to tell everyone
> that
>> there's nothing
>>> to say.

Ants crawl over leaves –
> I need to sweep the driveway clean.
>> I need to wash and wax the car.
>>> I need to wash these ants away.

I don't know how
> thistles got caught in my hair.
>> I combed them out – the ones which fell off
>>> scratched my face and my body.

The hairdresser said
> 'Let's add a warm colour.
>> Your skin is too pale
>>> for your dark hair.'

'I know,' I said,
> 'I keep my skin on a coat hanger at night.
>> I sleep in my bare bones
>>> so nothing can scratch it.'

'You're sad,' said a passer-by
> and another thistle fell off my hair.
>> 'I'm not,' I tell him, 'it's nothing.'
>>> This is a poem about nothing.

Rhetoric

I am
an eloquent
elegant
adamant
unsent letter.

Sacred

I learned not to trust
ancient oracles.
When they said 'love'
they inadvertently meant 'agape',
while worshippers bent,
kneeled and danced
hoping for the pagan 'eros'.

Sacred for me
is the smile of this girl
who's just met her boyfriend
in the neon-lit mall.

Teenagers at the movies

In the outside world
some thing or other is going on right now.
On the screen, heroes live out dramas.
In the last row a boy and a girl
carefully hold the moment
between their palms.

Free

Oysters wrap their hurt in pearl,
whales make love
between sheets of liquid silk,
the early full moon sheds its mask
into the ocean.

Song

In my garden I plant
coral reefs and volcanoes
and tired of colours
I water the weeds.
I've got a rune on my left eyelid –
on my right eyelid I keep
the kiss of a past lover.
I also limp a bit since I trod
on the luminous ray of a glow-worm.
On my ring finger I wear gossamer thread
and lizards are my earrings.

www.ingramcontent.com/pod-product-compliance
Lightning Source LLC
Chambersburg PA
CBHW062149100526
44589CB00014B/1750